*nature sounds
without nature sounds*

Sad Press
Bristol 2019

for everyone under the halo

Oolong

These days fill up with things to say:

all copper and candied fingers

The lemon-coloured wilderness

Do you believe, hello

This is my pollen song

preserving the undertow

patterning leaves

Lose a little space

for celadon

It's what we make of the sky

it's a concept

you can't monetise.

B minor

I have this recurring dream
where J.S. Bach stubs his cigarette
in the split womb of a geode
prior to composing a gorgeous rondeau
he's all like to Anna, fetch me the apricots
and she cuts up the sunset just for him
doling calorific cloud as though to a
starving godchild, softening
a thing to see
makes me leak milk into paintings
where licks of oil resemble cliffs
and colourless I come
back to see the acid in light repeat.

Prairie Score

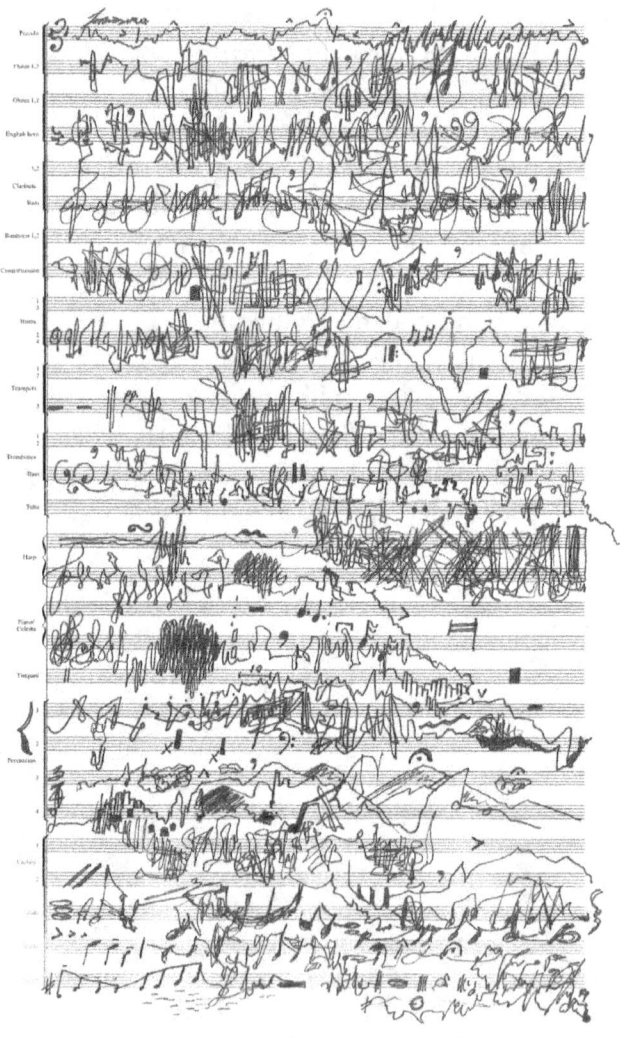

Lament

For now I am done with my warbling head,
these wasps in the dark make fricatives.
I don't want a bitterness of past, I just want to eat
the way our eyes met. Lou had said it was perfect
but he didn't know the world would end
right here, where you pause for breath:
all of the music leapt out of the zoo.
I remember we lived on stargaze phone calls
and the time of our tongues.
Here comes another apocalypse moon;
the landscape heaves tequila again.
Picture me blue: you extinguish a message
I shouldn't have sent. For now I am out
of the side of myself, folding pheremonal chord.
We share the abscess of a song it seems.

Fractal

The little red ants make love
on the patio outside the gallery
their beaded bodies click
and fall apart like glitches
too soon for me to scoop a line
and call it art

Because it takes effort, the art
dazzles to a brazen love
in the manner of shapes, a line
after line made way in the gallery
with intimations of glitches
that would split and click

Maybe the sunlight needs to click
back into gold the realist art
is a canvas of glitches
I try to unpick them each as love
because fucking in the gallery
is best when you fly on a line

Your gilded body on the line
I feel the discs of your spine now click
one by one around the gallery
the sound of our skin effects art
I want a postcard of this love
to slip into my jeans the glitches

As if kissing the space of these glitches
around the circular atrium line
I am in love
with each bone, those clicks
in the forest of all that is art
my favourite shadow of gallery

Foliage; our tiny voices like plaques in the gallery
I listen for you spreading the glitches
of surface and root, a hardened art
that crusts on each line
of a moment prolonged by click
after click, a clockwork love

Made silvery art in stippled glitches
your love of the gallery
its line in curvature; little red ants click into dust.

Rabbit by Proxy

Something is coming home, a cautious sonnet.
Laconic with chemistry, this sick day
endures a trace of sleep; you ask
how I've slept, you are lavish success.
Possessing a solvent thought I like, the voice
anointed with chrisms of land and sea,
a shale-made eden. I have resorted
this list of conditionals, by order of burrow
and terminal echo. You pulse close
but I am clean. We lost the auks and ospreys,
pressing soft ears to the soil. To say
"here we will be in a sheiling", deeply our sweet bass
scores the forest's insomnia; I let you in
and found myself scared of whoever remained.

Saucers of Mercury

Cleaving deep in your cool gestalt
at other levels, the cats are shining in marble epochs.

We traded painkillers wherever we could,
supplanting the higher solutions of angels

Our eyes now scattered in Mondrian hallways,
reflecting pools of lunar rain.

We blink back the satellites,
finding a fresh trypophobia universe.

There is a slow upheaval of sleep
consenting the breath of the others forever:

I see an actor cut lines on *Being and Time*,
a supermarket blue to vanish with you.

Melancholic

Why offer a punnet of ruined cherries?
No one will miss
us, disowning beloved exile
our limbs cross into triangles.

With everything, we get less specific.
There is disaster without release
and the other side;
I am trying to text you
a stem of the ending.

Animation matters less now,
you have pulled all shimmer from the screen
and wept without appetite;

I let myself go like a lantern.
This pain is irreversibly sweet. Imagine
what it's like not to know;
we simulate contingency
until our eyes spill ash.

The horizon was never a blush before us.

Oculus Riff

Here lies our nest of glass,
wherever the text goes scrolling
in back & forth ley lines of heat-clipped prose:
I thought I had a name, a dirty martini.
A year it took learning to listen,
fixing myself on special deals
and every Kandinsky adorning the walls of Pizza Hut
and every child's mute aria for time,
the seventeen minutes of ideals congealing
Time, is it lyric, you're alright at nice things:
the miniature click of video fingers,
Wildwood affairs, avocado on rye;
I'll come at you milky-eyed, the dull
liquidity catching hours
and something you broke last night
becomes anti-matter within the strobe;
this food is so fast, I love soda.
Every grid has its squint potential,
a metabolic laundry of deference
stirs in the powder. Turn over, let's try
this sideways. Would it take millions, waking up
all sweet for you, shooter to shooter.
Is this delirium in first-person?
They said the French word for mushroom

between the pass, Martyn Bennett's blackbirds
at some Spar & ever what ails us
in freezers, serrating
a shortcrust pastry with strawberry sundown
fattening days of here and yore.
Was it the centre of July, was it wild fire?
I'm a summer baby, yet silk among snowdrops
is cold to touch @ the Mermaid Motel,
some opening for splash magic: America is paradise.
I'll dwell in a condo, adjacent
to the cats of Jaffa, crunch my emotions
into quarts of ecstasy, purr. Call it coded emulsion
slicked upon windows. The buffering
threshold pressure of secrets. There is a treatise
and maybe a severed tail, a den, a schoolyard rhyme;
a stretch too far across the portal.
All wavy containment, full fathom file
a flat sarcophagus of photography:
isn't it kodachrome to forget
the burnup vertigo of the body in time?
Lay awhile still in the garden, subtracting
time's blush to memory's tint;
be that vague and often obvious.
Trust in this difference:
the sky could be translucent, a thirst,
evening the ache
of our crude black pupils.

Ariosos for Lavish Matter

1.
My self a disc I can't compact. Instead relay anecdotes
about the cost of waitressing in several nocturnal
glistenings; remember it was Coleridge
who could not walk because of hot milk
so my shame is a migraine deprived of opiates
and mostly I unravel my uniform
steaming beneath the lindens.

2.
In profile much prettier, every epoch
has its scary techne. Dream where my mother
reapplies lipstick in the restaurant mirror
and my life is the tiniest violet smudge at the edge.
Customers fill the sepulchral dark as other shadows
tuned to mystery, clearly
in pain with better quality, keep warm.

3.
Resisting the hot mathematics of football
downward to HD and popcorn memories, hum
of love and bike wheels. Honeycomb crunched
in the back of my mouth like a birthday.
These splintering words
to be dressed and buried, most of human
and more. A scalp massage is tentacle pleasure.

4.
Shouldn't we pick kin that resist us?
Dreadfully expensive, the wristwatch future
of light that lets in, silver fingers
threatening piano wires to whiter fire.
Tweets excepted, the lure of the bright
and Maytide familiar; remember he was
supposed to come play but didn't and hurt.

5.
An empathic blue sky, little organ donation
around the rain. In the red, the muscular
cumulus news fell away. Meat that thins
without freezing. I don't want to look
the way, this way. Cashing misery
for Mercury, cash in gin. Two cold halves
of a decent cut, fail to function as ritual.

6.
Hypothetical rhymes halo the bay,
become powder. How are we now.
The camera lifts the wax from your eyelids
startling a blankness of planetary lashes.
No sweet work of skin was sufficient,
those silhouette girls with faraway poses.
Switch off the desert, I'm not listening.

7.
Rub my eyes around the fantasy cedar
as if the sap stopped happening.
Hydraulic thought as all the rage
and wasting, most citizen damage
dismisses the winterized lanterns.
One line follows the next, a nest
curling up tight the language of saplings.

8.
In crispest best, street clover pales
to lilac assets; too true of an elevator birth
between ages. Starved in the dark
the poem's gloaming is a hollow in the elm
of my belly, not to sprawl any longer
the vitamin lore of extroversion. I require
such luxury of inherited messages.

9.
So maybe Meredith's hereditary spells
crested the gleaming sea's chartreuse, reductress
of cool semesters. Exceptionally latent
the corridor of aesthetic residues
repainted a glorious yellow.
All premonitions ring with red:
a seagull eating a seagull.

10.
Interrupted outlook is late-night, tricyclic
opening your mailbox for ravens. Advertise
a fresh electronic duo, treat us confidentially:
our slick new remix made the radio.
This addiction can wait till Friday, as I add
to my nerves undigested iron. No condition.
Popping kelp didn't help, am I yet shining.

11.
Halfway to Brunswick and back
in lossy compression of monochrome era. Missing
you much in abandoned houses, cloistered green.
Nothing a shake of desiccated opals won't fix
when the sparkler goes, death as fizz and cravings.
Some sort of wartime cousin now a chocolatier
and I really don't know what to say,
ready salted with these read receipts.

12.
My womb through the night was shredding
to suffer the sheets as glass
and the body's luminosity, I'd say
the wrought metallic twang of the tongue.
I pay for everything
and the recipe stays central
to rich boys, coke and brand new menus.

13.
Can I fetch you anything while I'm here?
How was it this time. The cervical curve
of bone at the brink of the plate, a balance
I exact as gravity. What sorts of eternity
do we choose for our labour?
I was so afraid of orange, poverty; your eyes
if they opened just so, like beautiful eggs.

14.
It didn't take long to recreate
the opaque catatonia of sad hospitality; news of aniseed
drained the pool. No-one came.
Chalked up to biospheric sequence
and now receding. Is there bread with that.
I spent ten minutes sketching to change things.
Remember you can always sleep.

15.
Didn't I say a dairy-free dream
would deliver me strange to some home or another.
When everything grew too green
and the smell of the bluebells
still deep in your neck like a song.
A sort of Gaussian moment propels me, lullaby ever
of red-berried February, the alkaloid.

16.
Coltan imbues each blade
of archival lust upon airplanes. A touch.
Some other pixelated dryad could plumb
matter from the web of a spider; my primary
accent dissolved as sand then ambient.
Each window of night became complicated,
pasteurised. I could not acquire the nascent tinder.

17.
Fluorescence rises from the woods
to a clearing of gilded tips, expiry dates, essays.
These demented lands where I love you
in the drafted webpage, a fractal
synapse unsampled. Our hours as baskets
of moulding fruit, glitching seeds. This can happen.
I like the loops of your voice, dust, the trivial starlings.

Modern Pop

The mango ad brought me here
phasing from the same double take

I could do with some juice now

Falling between changes in tempo
just sit on my breakfast
at varispeed

Slight continuum of pitch
brittle with trails

Make your talent wear something else
stripes are too tricky for digital.

Espeon

Psychic-type, easy to pine in the wild
for the instant, cash aurora
edible sun shard

Wherever we lurk
solastalgia happens online.

That closure came away like a colour.

Synchronicity of flesh and gemstone;
places we knelt in the dust
to retrieve our sacred berries.

Wearing critical velvet
I share a trait with no evolution;
this is what it is to see through anything.

Solaris

These days of languishing matter:

equal melodic
try not, tectonic
try not to—

The way you make ash
out of language

Some other order retreats,
tweest foliage

softening a school walk home with lambs' ears,
amnesia

I wish I could speak
the words that choose me
coming everywhere green like aphids

The way you make ash
into language

Here on the pavement, the sheets
pullover grey
a birthday left of maybe, flaking
Nothing more warm,
you're inside a planet, the one that's inside you;
must everything always be crawling

Mostly waxen blades of ocean
mostly a thought

Soldered, the lamp is core;
I turned you.

Whole new palettes of sky,
an elder range;
I keep asking my phone
to remember the good things.

2009

Last summer of love without credit(s)
chasing common varieties:
nudist cloud, plant food, scotrail blue

Fizzing stars on my palm
you swore were edible
drawing bloody austerity

I try you for bath salts
watching the screen of the centre melt
as if already twice-balearic

Video come back,
the lake is a vice of attitude air.

Insomnia Song

With echo, the length of a drastic silk
unfurls from itself. In optimism
there is a loop which sings, clearly
until the close of a swift duration.

The mode of the tape was shadow
and some of it passed our quieted lips
with euphemism. I enter
the crest of a bittersweet room

With the walls just bibliographies.
What you get here, you get better
on the surface of milk. What gives
of the air is a pixel ache;

A new development in icicles required us.
In my schism of knitwear,
permission to crawl beside Judith
granted. I took a lot of light from you:

Long have I suffered the intimate orchid.
How about the floor, softly
astride itself? Here we click.
Tiny babies in sleep belong to no-one.

Clearing

What gives, no air
is reply; I speak to the Spotify gods
who know me,
the iconic thought
settles in green for connection.
If everything pure, no, have you turned
the lights off for me
I wake in this way, the trains
shudder hard around your bed.
I laughed so hard I cried at the lamb
and the plastic eternity beside
the downloaded album

My sweet app, does your transference
become us better?
Whichever it is, bring me a tune
and I will say of the dark
this is not my countryside
warming the tongue of a lyric
this is not my beautiful fur
of a dog of a wolf of a garden.
This is excepted, you mumble
the same fuck that comes in us better

As stones, and geometry
secretes its truth to me, a plainer mileage
The way you arranged my novella, two
towers of narrative, a little seducing insect
between us

When we survive the heat

This endless matinee hair, a monochrome drape
I can hear in the windows all of my real
I can hear in the windows all of my sky
too loud to get out, we stay in the tower
I have said, do you choose Berlin or the prairie?

It is so blue the cows come home
for their milkier nudity

Lanugo versions of
famished sleep; I like that

Everything rose is a painting of realist
eclipse, don't panic
my spidery jaw, my veil of eye

I run around your face again
The cows come back for your face again
Everything here is a film, a small recalcitrant
act of perplex

You ache, you bear your mother's antlers

Come round now, blank of iris
until we are blue
I hear in your gaze the same clean whistle
I hear in the simple
weather a thought

Where streets are glossaries
just as rich, tumbled
tooth-bitten architects stay here
everything soft just stays here

Hey, did you see the radio start to listen
and the lambs come home to the long
cow movie, that rested its laurels on so much sunset
the credits forgot to roll
like confession

It was a good thing you brought the receipt
Lucid, most of our animals now
can do that

Look the way you would down a straw

And the planet sucks off the rain
imagine the poem was a playlist

You ache inside me, easy to say
true green: watch whatever andromeda wants
and she is as fatherless
in starry sequel as me
on the golf course, eating my air again

They add up to shinies, and everything
you scratch off with your thumb
until the silver shows through
and the song—

This was the forest,
because of your bone
and the iconic click

For desktop canopies
away a kiss. Trust
they said of psydust,
extra lichen
to soften the noise of the walls
without bees

You cost bluest like milk
and too much of us, there in the aisle
I feel a special breeze
and the name of the inbox is rainbow
and the collapse
I felt elsewhere was possible

Switch off as you will, wholesome
shone my agnostic death
which failed as
the moth
that flew
into the fridge
say missile, we breathe

Super lovely the cry again,
its screen and the shape of the clarity, clarity

I entered a weight
And the song began
The same reply. It was nice
to see the shaky news, to really
connect a love that way; however
sorry I am for the airbrush everyone,
you have seen what it means to me

Algorithmically speaking, okay,
now you have witnessed the moon in business

Did you find what you furrowed
of a needed season
bowl of oranges, oily clearing;
I got carried away with the vines again
I made of these folders a want, a livestock.

Subtractive Classics Vol. 7

Gold bubbles raising the question of *us*:
a single sunset sip
for global analgesia

As if we did not want this to end
all anorexia oracular

Walk without solar clause, you are premium
air and bone.

The world just turns, as if it forgot
its evil. Lethargic enchantress
pull me together

From injury, we exist still;
our vitamin weather
haemorrhages techno

Here in my petrichor secret.

Evie

There is a time ahead. It is the same
hour we have of this, portion
that is life. Considering

The sensibility of the sea
we take vogue of a marinal fabric,
blue drapes that move silently

Across the glamour
of dawn; her derelict
existence knows us best.

I cannot help
reaching for skylines:
this gestural end

That means anything
of the body, salt, reel to rain;
a particular reset.

Acknowledgements

The title of this pamphlet is a quote from Bernie Brooks' *Quietus* review of Hiro Kone's 2018 LP, *Pure Expenditure*.

Cover design ('*aquaria*') is by Finn Arschavir.

'Ariosos for Lavish Matter' was previously published in *Blackbox Manifold* and 'Oolong' and 'Melancholic' in *Stride*, with many thanks to the editors.

Thank you to Colin, Daisy, Dom and Katy for reading drafts of these poems, and as ever to my comrades at SPAM.

www.ingramcontent.com/pod-product-compliance
Lightning Source LLC
Chambersburg PA
CBHW071509080526
44587CB00016B/2731